One Minute Prayers™

FOR *Busy Moms*

Text by Hope Lyda

HARVEST HOUSE PUBLISHERS

EUGENE, OREGON

ONE-MINUTE PRAYERS is a series trademark of The Hawkins Children's LLC. Harvest House Publishers, Inc., is the exclusive licensee
of the trademark ONE-MINUTE PRAYERS.

ONE-MINUTE PRAYERS™ FOR BUSY MOMS
Copyright © 2004 by Harvest House Publishers
Eugene, Oregon 97402
www.harvesthousepublishers.com

ISBN 0-7369-1284-3

Printed in the United States of America

04 05 06 07 08 09 10 11 12   / BP-CF /   10 9 8 7 6 5 4 3

Contents

Expect a Miracle

The creation waits in eager expectation for the sons of God to be revealed. For the creation was subjected to frustration, not by its own choice, but by the will of the one who subjected it, in hope that the creation itself will be liberated from its bondage to decay and brought into the glorious freedom of the children of God.

ROMANS 8:19-21

∼

As I awaited the birth of my child, Lord, I was worried about the process. Was everything in order for this to go smoothly? Did anyone and everyone involved know exactly what they were doing…because I didn't. It was not about perfection; it was about fear. My eager anticipation had turned to anxiety. Overflowing with life, my worrying self forgot to turn to the Creator of life.

How You must have tried to get my attention. But I was focused. I saw only the task ahead. And then the day came, and my sweet child was placed in my arms. I forgot about the process and embraced the miracle. My spirit, once restricted by fear, was liberated by the gift of Your hope.

Each time I look at my growing child, Lord, I am reminded to expect a miracle.

Quiet

In the Quiet

The quiet words of the wise are more to be heeded than the shouts of a ruler of fools.

ECCLESIASTES 9:17

∾

When the world was conceived, the rush of creation, the rush of quiet, the rush of perfection must have been awesome. Lord, take me to that moment in time. Replace images of man's power with visions of Your power. God, help me see what You want me to see in my life.

When my children's voices fill my every waking moment, I forget what a blessing they are. I let my ears glide over the surface of their chatter, and I miss the words You speak to me through them. Encourage my spirit to seek quiet, to reenergize, and to become healthy and aware. This I owe to my children, but also I owe it to myself as Your child.

Trading Busyness for Peace

Make it your ambition to lead a quiet life.

1 THESSALONIANS 4:11

ᢙ

Grant me a moment of quiet today, Lord. I might find it in unexpected places. It might be a time when I would rather be busy or stay distracted. But coax me into Your peace. Direct my mind to thoughts of You, my family, those who need prayer.

Calm my anxieties about the risk of slowing down, doing nothing. I will step into the quiet and feel the relief from busyness. Like a star suspended in the heavens, I will bow to Your peace.

Come with Me

Then, because so many people were coming and going that they did not even have a chance to eat, he said to them, "Come with me by yourselves to a quiet place and get some rest."

MARK 6:31

∽

From the moment I wake up until my last goodnights, there is noise to fill my head and spirit. I hear requests. Demands. Instructions. Pleas. And that is on top of my own thought life. Lord, call me away from all of this. My heart desires to be with You. Lead me to a quiet place.

Lord, You call me by name. You prepare a place of quiet and restoration. When I enter this time of prayer, You are waiting to embrace me, hold me up, and offer me strength for my journey. I have such hunger, Lord. And You offer nourishment and a place to rest my weary soul.

Rest Before Sleep

This is what the LORD says to me: "I will remain quiet and will look on from my dwelling place, like shimmering heat in the sunshine, like a cloud of dew in the heat of harvest."

ISAIAH 18:4

∾

Now I lay me down to sleep.... Lord, each evening I check on my children before I lie down. Just minutes after their pre-bedtime battle, they are now peaceful; their breathing is full and trusting. This sight calms me. My tight shoulders and the knots of worried thoughts loosen. I feel free to reflect on the day You have given me and to wonder about what You have for me tomorrow.

Now I can release my hold on those things I cannot control. I regret any resistance I had today to Your will. I know that peace comes to those living in Your way. In the wake of my battle for control, my breathing is full and trusting. Thank You, Lord.

Change

Change of Heart

*Change your laughter to mourning and your joy to
gloom. Humble yourselves before the Lord, and he
will lift you up.*

JAMES 4:9-10

❧

Experiencing the intense joy of children has also
opened up life to the possibility of great loss, Lord.
Behind smiles of deep happiness, I worry. I encourage
my children to step out, to try new things—all the
while my heart is racing, evaluating the risk of physical or emotional hurts.

I believe this new depth of feeling is a gift from
You. Never has my heart been so open, so vulnerable,
and so full. I understand how You must feel watching
all of Your children as they struggle, learn to love, and
grow in Your will. When I imagine the sorrow of ever
losing my family, Lord, call me to cherish the immense
joy of today. Thank You for changing my life to en-
compass such passion.

A Different Outlook

He called a little child and had him stand among them. And he said: "I tell you the truth, unless you change and become like little children, you will never enter the kingdom of heaven."

MATTHEW 18:2-3

≈

Motherhood has taught me so much, Lord. You must laugh while watching the way my once perfectly scheduled, finely orchestrated life has been thrown off-kilter. Sometimes I beg to return to those days. I remember being a punctual person. I recall leaving the house confident that I did *not* have oatmeal on my sleeve. There was a time I cruised the grocery store without having to count the number of tiles in each aisle or the rolls of toilet paper on the shelf.

And just when I miss my past freedoms, You remind me to become *more* like a little child. I hear this, Lord, and pay attention to matters of great importance as well as to daily minutiae, because all of it creates this wonderful life You have given to me. I am no longer preoccupied with the law of social perfection. Even when I have chocolate on my face, You first see the clean, innocent heart inside me.

Renewed by Your Power

*Praise be to the name of God for ever and ever;
wisdom and power are his. He changes times and seasons; he sets up kings and deposes them. He gives
wisdom to the wise and knowledge to the dis-
cerning.*

DANIEL 2:20-21

❧

God, I need a miracle today. Just one. An itty-bitty
change of heart. That is all. But I know it will take
Your mighty hand to fill me with grace. Grace enough
for the busy day ahead of me. An okay morning took
a sharp turn during a breakfast serving of bickering
among the children. Lord, please change my heart.
Impress upon my mind the affection You hold for Your
children. I want to carry this with me as my model for
the day.

You see the shadows that fall upon my spirit when
days go bad. Help me watch for the blessings that exist
between the inconveniences or irritations. Mold my
words so that they are uplifting and encouraging. I
praise You, Lord. Your love is so powerful; it changes
the course of a woman's heart.

Never Wavering

Therefore, my dear brothers, stand firm. Let nothing move you. Always give yourselves fully to the work of the Lord, because you know that your labor in the Lord is not in vain.

1 CORINTHIANS 15:58

❧

Change can give birth to the miraculous. I watch my children grow inside and out. They absorb information and form concepts and beliefs. They even seek You and love You. But, Lord, there are times when I try to pass off my inconsistent behavior as a change of opinion or perspective. I give in to the whims of my children when I should stay true to the guidelines my husband and I have agreed on. Yet, You call me to stand firm in my belief, my understanding of truth. Please help me when I hedge slightly left or right of honesty, integrity, and love.

As I take liberties with my family's house rules, my children take notes. They are piecing together the image of a life under Your authority. May I not forget this. Help me show them a worthy example. Let my path be straight, my stance firm, and my gaze steady.

Gifts

The Fruit of Your Faithfulness

Every good and perfect gift is from above, coming down from the Father of the heavenly lights, who does not change like shifting shadows. He chose to give us birth through the word of truth, that we might be a kind of firstfruits of all he created.

JAMES 1:17-18

∽

You bless me, Lord, with many gifts. As I look at the course my life has taken, Your hand is evident every step of the way. From the time Your word gave birth to my soul, I have lived a rich life. I regret the times when doubt filled my mind during a difficult circumstance. I understand now how patience reveals Your faithfulness in all things.

I pray today for faith in Your unchanging ways. I flit about with human fickleness, casting shadows on the path of truth You have laid out for me. I will regain my footing on the solidity of gratitude. And here I will see the gifts fall from heaven.

A Humble Request

If you, then, though you are evil, know how to give
good gifts to your children, how much more will
your Father in heaven give good gifts to those who
ask him!

MATTHEW 7:11

∽

My children relate to gifts with varying grace.
Sometimes there is little appreciation. They make
requests boldly and hold out their hands, waiting for
me to comply. In a moment of shyness they will lower
their eyes and voice and vaguely state a need...hoping
I will understand how to solve their problem, fill their
void.

Lord, I know that I do not approach You with great
consistency. But as my heart opens wide to the needs
of my children, I have a glimpse of Your desire to
bestow good gifts on those who call out to You. I will
try to ask in humility, never demanding, but always
with an outreached hand to receive the love You offer.
Because no matter what supplication my lips might
stumble over, it is Your love that fills the void in my
heart.

Answering the Call

For God's gifts and his call are irrevocable.

ROMANS 11:29

∽

Lord, I thank You for the abilities, direction, and talents You have given me. These strengths balance out my areas of weakness. They help me serve my family and those with whom I come in contact. Recognizing my strengths allows me to become a helpmate to my husband.

Yet I admit there are times when I view these gifts as burdens. Forgive me when I am reluctant to develop these areas in my life, or when I have ignored Your leading. Help me pray even when I am busy. Guide me to say yes to those activities where my gifts can serve You. I long to embrace Your call and become a vessel that overflows with Your goodness.

Looking for a Handout

All these people gave their gifts out of their wealth;
but she out of her poverty put in all she had to live on.

LUKE 21:4

∽

I am poor today, Lord. Poor in spirit ... and lacking strength. I know my children see it. They look at me with expectation, hoping I will snap out of it in time to care for them properly. I was doing fine and then hit a wall. Truth is, I have been running on memories of when I had energy and on temporary, fabricated strength-givers like caffeine and junk food.

I am sorry it has taken me this long to come to You. Lord, I pray for Your strength right now. Let the gifts that come out of my poverty be a blessing to my children. May they become a testimony of Your power. When You fill my spirit and You replenish my will and desire, I am wealthy.

Rest

Secure in Your Arms

*Let the beloved of the L*ORD *rest secure in him, for he shields him all day long, and the one the L*ORD *loves rests between his shoulders.*

DEUTERONOMY 33:12

❧

Hold me, Lord. Oh, how I need to rest. My days have been so scattered. I call some of them productive, and in some I am just acting out the daily grind...but all leave me weary and longing for comfort. As I wipe the forehead of a feverish child or bend down close to tender ears to whisper good night, I sense Your healing touch and soothing words.

Lead me to quiet times of meditation and calm. My body is so tired; I must lean on You throughout the day. And You are always there. Thank You, Lord, for picking up this child, cradling my heart, and offering rest for my soul.

Looking to You

The LORD replied, "My Presence will go with you, and
I will give you rest."

EXODUS 33:14

∽

I am a bit afraid of the road ahead. I see a curve, some distant signs, and a shady outline of things to come. That is too vague for me. My family and I need security, not more uncertainty. This fear of the unknown draws energy from me. I have been short with people whom I love, Lord.

Direct my eyes to Yours so that I do not lose sight of my future. Remove my fear with the promise of eternity. Do not let me forget, during this stretch of days without definition, that You are with me. My soul will be rested as I turn the corner and clearly see the way to go.

Mercy Wrapped in Truth

This then is how we know that we belong to the truth, and how we set our hearts at rest in his presence whenever our hearts condemn us. For God is greater than our hearts, and he knows everything.

1 JOHN 3:19-20

᧞

Guilt covers me like a thick woolen blanket in the heat of summer. It scratches my skin. It makes me thirsty. I will promise anything to have it removed so I can breathe. Why do I suffocate under the weight of unnecessary restraints? The promise that sets me free is not one I will make; it is Your promise of forgiveness. It is Your truth that peels away layers of guilt and shame.

You are greater than my heart, with its debilitating perception of burden. You free me and give me room to breathe. The coolness of Your mercy quenches my spirit's thirst, and I am able to rest in Your grace.

Returning to Sabbath

*For six days, work is to be done, but the seventh day
is a Sabbath of rest, holy to the LORD.*

EXODUS 31:15

❧

We have forgotten how to rest, Lord. Other cultures take siestas, have long summers meant for leisure or vacation, and establish reasonable workdays that make room for meals and family. I have bought into a nonstop lifestyle, and I am tired of it. Lord, remove my notions that a rigid, busy day is a productive one. May I be fruitful, but may I no longer sacrifice moments of prayer, meditation, and laughter because they are not on the schedule.

I won't throw out my planner...it provides security and order for me. But I will become a steward of my time so the gift of Sabbath returns to my lifestyle. Open up my life to the comfort of rest. You speak to us when we are quiet. I commit to meeting You in stillness this week. It is a start.

Growth

Standing Tall

Even youths grow tired and weary, and young men stumble and fall; but those who hope in the LORD will renew their strength.

ISAIAH 40:30-31

∽

I warn my children about their limits all the time. "You will get tired if you carry those toys to the playground." "Your feet will blister if you wear those new shoes without socks." "Staying up too late will make tomorrow unbearable." And I am right almost every time. Yet, am I listening to Your words of wisdom for my life? Have I matured in my faith enough to walk a steady, straight path?

In a quest for control, I carry too much, don't I? I proceed into situations without the protection of prayer. I let myself run too hard, too long, and I make myself and other people miserable. So today I sit and listen to You. I await Your instruction for my day. And I sit a bit taller, straighter . . . like a wise person of faith.

Rising Toward Heaven

I made you grow like a plant of the field. You grew up and developed and became the most beautiful of jewels.

EZEKIEL 16:7

∽

They grow like weeds! My relatives say this about my children, and I must laugh. They do indeed. Their lengthening limbs tangle and intertwine at awkward stages, stretch and wave at more poetic ages. They flower into new beings all the time.

Lord, You have watched me sprout up from the days of my youth. What stage am I in right now? In the whirl of my life, I seldom can judge if I am twisting or dancing. Am I fading or blossoming? I pray that You find me and my life beautiful and pleasing, Lord. The more I grow up, the more I desire to be Your child… at any stage.

Growing Pains

But grow in the grace and knowledge of our Lord and Savior Jesus Christ. To him be glory both now and forever!

2 PETER 3:18

✒

My children bring home interesting and more advanced homework every year. I want to tell them that life presents even tougher lessons. I hear them speak of dreams and goals with excitement. My first thoughts are clouded with warnings of possible disappointments, unexpected changes, or unrealistic dreams. Lord, I don't want to think these thoughts when in the presence of their enthusiasm and belief.

As Your child, I know that the mysteries of life are awesome and wonderful. Don't let me forget what You have done and can do with my days. Immerse me in Your grace and knowledge. Return to me a hunger and passion. My life will bring You glory only when I let go of my regrets and grow in my faith.

Harvesttime

The seed will grow well, the vine will yield its fruit,
the ground will produce its crops, and the heavens
will drop their dew. I will give all these things as an
inheritance to the remnant of this people.

ZECHARIAH 8:12

∽

My growth follows the order of Your creation. You craft every seed and vine; You mold the shape of my heart and soul. And You know the shape my life will take in the future. I may act like I know what I am doing and where I am going, but You are aware of my insecurities. Give me guidance in all areas.

Do not let me become too comfortable in my present state of being. I want to sip of heaven's dew and be nourished by Your favor. I pray for a wise spirit that leads me to new challenges and opportunities for growth. Do not let me wither on this vine called life.

Motherhood

My Heavenly Parent

As a mother comforts her child, so will I comfort you.

ISAIAH 66:13

∽

Lord, You teach me the ways of motherhood. Your gentle touch comforts me. Your precepts direct me. And Your commands keep my steps firmly on the path You make for me. There are days when I feel like I am faking motherhood, or that I have started a round of "playing house" that will not end.

On days like today, when I don't know if I can pretend one more minute, You give me a gift. A child calls out, seeking my love. I mend a broken heart and fix a broken bike. And You remind me that my version of motherhood is real. And although I am not perfect, I am real. May my motherhood reflect the love of my heavenly parent.

It's About Respect

Honor your father and your mother, as the LORD your God has commanded you, so that you may live long and that it may go well with you in the land the LORD your God is giving you.

DEUTERONOMY 5:16

✌

Lord, mold me into a mother worthy of honor. I cannot force my children to respect me, but I can live a life that is fruitful, deeply rooted in Your truth, and overflowing with Your love. I vow to bring my children up in a godly way. I will honor my husband because he is deserving and because this models respect in our home.

How wonderful that You desire life to go well for me...for my children...for all Your children. You are a merciful, kind, and giving God. Let me lead my children into the promised land You prepare for us.

Correct Me If I'm Wrong

Teach me, and I will be quiet; show me where I have been wrong.

JOB 6:24

᪥

Correct me, Lord. When You see me acting out or acting up, correct my ways. When I discipline my children, I fear they do not sense the love behind my stern voice or pointed finger. But the love is there, and it is so deep. I think of this when I hear Your words of correction, or when You guide my steps with the force of an unexpected happening. Help me sense Your deep love for me during these times.

Motherhood is all about the practice and discipline of love. Thank You for being my example, Lord. You want only the best for me. I want only the best for my children. Teach me, and show me where I have been wrong.

Becoming Me

Our people must learn to devote themselves to doing what is good, in order that they may provide for daily necessities and not live unproductive lives.

TITUS 3:14

∽

As a child, I had many visions of what I might become. "What do you want to be when you grow up?" was a question I welcomed. My answer changed nearly every time. I prayed for You to bless my choice of the day. Now that I am a mother, I understand what it is to be committed to a vision, a purpose. You have given me this clarity.

I have other responsibilities and hold other positions, but motherhood is an act of devotion. I care for my family and provide for their needs. I build them up with truths from Your Word. When it is dark, I point to Your light. And when my children dream of becoming something special, I pray You will bless their choice of the day.

Life

The Good Life

*Surely goodness and love will follow me all the days
of my life, and I will dwell in the house of the LORD
forever.*

PSALM 23:6

✑

La dolce vita, the sweet life. To me, this phrase
defines the Christian life. It is a rich existence based
upon a foundation of grace and goodness. Lord, help
me to taste the sweetness of my days, to sip from a cup
of divine nectar. When my attitude or immediate circumstances turn sour, let me wave unpleasantries
aside and embrace the flavorful, abundant life.

Thank You for filling my heart with hope's promise. I am fortunate, happy, and joyful because I reside
in Your house forever.

The Ups and Downs

Guard my life and rescue me; let me not be put to shame, for I take refuge in you.

PSALM 25:20

∽

I stumbled over my arrogance. I spoke when silence was much more appropriate. I didn't hurt anyone, but I made a fool of myself. And I didn't reflect Your goodness. Still, You picked me up and let me continue. But the sting of humiliation can be felt long past an awkward moment of failure.

Lord, protect me from my own selfish whimsy. Calm my mind so that I think and pray first, and then consider silence or caution an option. It would be nice to not require Your refuge so often, but in the meantime may other people forget my indiscretions and recall only my Redeemer.

Life's Riches

A man's riches may ransom his life, but a poor man hears no threat.

PROVERBS 13:8

∽

I am surrounded by elements of bondage, Lord. Material wealth, modern conveniences, advanced technology…these evidences of achievement anchor me to the earth and the world's ways. Anyone or any one misfortune could hold my life hostage by threatening the safety and future of these empty "things." Why do I place so much emphasis on the accrual and maintenance of such trappings?

Free my mind so I do not fear poverty, Lord. Give me the wisdom to release false needs and replace them with attitudes a servant requires. As I fall to my knees, prosperity's hold on me falls away. I am not threatened by possible destruction or destitution. My wealth flows from a limitless source: Your grace.

A Covenant to Create

*I will remember my covenant between me and you
and all living creatures of every kind. Never again
will the waters become a flood to destroy all life.*

GENESIS 9:15

∽

Lord, I hold Your promises so close to my heart.
When the world fails me, I have faith in Your love.
When I perceive the floodwaters rising, let me stand confidently on the foundation of Your covenant.

Out my kitchen window I see evidence of Your
commitment to create and not to destroy. I am thankful for nature's beauty. The aesthetics and intricacies
are wondrous. But it is the abundance of Your creation
that reminds me how much You love life.

Needs

Sigh of the Times

All my longings lie open before you, O Lord; my sighing is not hidden from you.

PSALM 38:9

∽

Lately I have been sighing a lot—too much. I frown upon this generic expression of disappointment when my children force out their breath at the dinner table, heave their chests when ground rules have been set, and roll their eyes for emphasis once I reprimand their behavior. Yet in my prayers to You, I have been sighing. At first it is just an expression of fatigue. But over time it becomes a sign of discontentment. This attitude says, "You have failed me, Lord. You have not met my deepest needs."

Forgive me, Lord, for this behavior. Erase my disappointment and take hold of my life. Embed righteous longings deep within my soul. Let my sighs be replaced by songs of Your wondrous plans.

Serving the Needs of the Lord

Those who were sent ahead went and found it just as he had told them. As they were untying the colt, its owners asked them, "Why are you untying the colt?" They replied, "The Lord needs it."

LUKE 19:32-34

✍

"What do You need, Lord?" This is not a question I ask too often or even think to pray about. I focus on my needs whenever a listening ear is made available. I know You are almighty, all-powerful, and therefore do not require my assistance to accomplish anything, but just the same...what can I do for You today, Lord?

Have You been asking for an extra hand recently? A family across town needs help to make ends meet. One of my children's friends craves encouragement. My husband longs for me to really hear his hopes and dreams. I am here, Lord. Please guide me, and use me to fulfill Your plan.

More than Lip Service

If one of you says to him, "Go, I wish you well; keep warm and well fed," but does nothing about his physical needs, what good is it? In the same way, faith by itself, if it is not accompanied by action, is dead.

JAMES 2:16-17

≈

Lord, I gave someone the brush-off recently, and I feel bad. Forgive me for dismissing a very genuine and deep need because I was in a hurry. Lord, remind me of the blessings in my life, all of which are from You. Remind me I do not make it through any day without the kindness of other people. Remind me of grace.

Stop me before I actually speak those simple phrases that rise in my throat, such as: "I hope you feel better." "If that becomes a big problem, let me know." "I'm sure it will get better." "God will work it out." Turn my platitudes into "How can I serve you?"—an expression of Your active grace. Inspire me to reach out to other people in a meaningful way.

Getting over Myself

The LORD *will guide you always; he will satisfy your needs in a sun-scorched land and will strengthen your frame.*

ISAIAH 58:11

∽

My daily prayers seem to revolve around my needs. I am blinded by them. I can go for days and just wallow in them. Do You tire of my selfish rants? I do. I fill our quiet moments with a long list of requirements. I feel like I give to other people so much during my day. They are people I love, but the act of giving takes so much. By the time I fall before You, I am bursting with *my* needs, *my* wants, *my* longings in life.

I am right to go to You, Lord, to fill my needs. But give me a heart for the needs of other people. Lead me to a place of praise and worship so I can express my love for You. And help me to see how much I am receiving in those times of giving.

Worry

When Hearts Talk

Therefore do not worry about tomorrow, for tomorrow will worry about itself. Each day has enough trouble of its own.

MATTHEW 6:34

∽

I like to listen to my children's nighttime prayers. When I hear their voices lifted up to You, I am gaining a glimpse of their hearts, their concerns, and their worries. I understand what preoccupies those active minds through words that surface as soon as they fold their hands and bow their heads. I see the relief and release cross their faces when they say "Amen."

Is this what happens when I pray? Do You see a vulnerable heart willing to share its fears? Or have I forgotten how to really talk to You? Lord, strip me of my clichéd petitions and prayers of thanksgiving. Let me bow down before my Lord and tell You about my worries. Let me give these over to You like a trusting child.

Ready or Not

But make up your mind not to worry beforehand
how you will defend yourselves. For I will give you
words and wisdom that none of your adversaries
will be able to resist or contradict.

LUKE 21:14-15

∽

I cannot help it. I get defensive. I'm a worrier,
Lord. You have heard my prayers throughout the day
and know how much I stew over what will happen
next, what someone will say, what my response will
be. It is exhausting. I pray for peace during these
times. I pray that I will trust You implicitly with each
and every situation I face.

Lord, let me feed on Your Word and Your wisdom.
Let it fall from my lips at the right moment. May I
never take my faith in You and twist it into arrogance,
but allow me the peace that is born of trust. Today,
Lord, I will not waste one minute fretting.

In Your Time

Humble yourselves, therefore, under God's mighty hand, that he may lift you up in due time. Cast all your anxiety on him because he cares for you.

1 PETER 5:6-7

∽

I asked my husband to fix the kitchen door about five times, Lord. It is still broken. Now I am obsessed with this imperfection. If it isn't one thing, it is another. I distort the importance of a simple problem, when the real situation that needs fixing is ignored.

Lord, You know how my heart needs to be healed. You know each relationship that is strained or torn. Release me from anxiety and anger. I bow down beneath Your hand and pray for You to fix my brokenness in Your time. I pray I will be in Your presence and following Your way when You are ready to lift me up.

Joy After the Storm

*When anxiety was great within me, your consolation
brought joy to my soul.*

PSALM 94:19

∾

When waves of worry crash down on me, I look for
refuge in Your arms. Your embrace is strong and certain, and You lift me high above the roar of concern.
The safety of Your firm grip allows me to release my fears
into the air. Worries of yesterday drift downward like
gentle raindrops.

The storm that threatened my life, my sanity, my
happiness is now transformed. In the mist I see the
colors of the rainbow, and my anxiety turns to joy. You
are amazing, Lord. You bring radiance to a darkened
soul. I hope I learn from this intimate encounter with
Your grace. As soon as a storm begins to brew within
me, I will seek Your peace.

Future

Sorrow Introduces Hope

There is surely a future hope for you, and your hope will not be cut off.

PROVERBS 23:18

∽

There is a future hope in You, Lord. When today feels dark, there is hope. When I pray for my children's future, there is hope. Your gift of tomorrow surrounds me and covers me. Hard times ground me deeper in Your promises. I cling to them so tightly. Lord, show me my past...the times when sorrow visited my life. In these times my faith was formed, defined, and strengthened.

Let me not waste those past moments of refinement. Let me turn to the faith You are growing in me as I face my future...a future of hope.

Building on a Right Spirit

Your beginnings will seem humble, so prosperous will your future be.

JOB 8:7

❦

Mine is a simple life. Extremely busy, yes. But still, my authentic needs are straightforward. I want my family to be healthy, loving, and walking in Your way. Personally, I want to be useful and kind. Humble my spirit, dear God, and purify my heart. Empty me of selfish ambition. Fill me with an enduring spirit.

I wait patiently for whatever You have for me. The simpler my life is now, the more obvious Your directions will be when change, pursuit, or silence are in order. May my life remain uncluttered so it becomes a worthy foundation for the future.

My Child's Future

*Consider the blameless, observe the upright; there is
a future for the man of peace.*

PSALM 37:37

∾

Lord, help me raise peace-filled children who will
become peace-loving adults. It is not easy to filter out
the world's violence and tendency toward insensitive
self-preservation. When examples of evil enter our
lives, let us pray over them. Help me to teach my children a godly approach to worldly problems.

I pray for my children and the future they will
walk through. May their hope always be placed in
You. And may I instruct my children in the ways of love.
This is the future I see for them.

The Gift for Generations

Let this be written for a future generation, that a people not yet created may praise the LORD: "The LORD looked down from his sanctuary on high, from heaven he viewed the earth, to hear the groans of the prisoners and release those condemned to death."

PSALM 102:18-20

❧

Mired in the details of today, I can forget what a gift the future is for myself and my family. There will be generations to follow in our steps. Lord, I pray for future members of my lineage who will serve You and carry faith into the future. You will offer them the same grace. Your gift does not change. May there always be ears to hear the message of Your salvation and may there always be hearts to receive its hope.

I take comfort in knowing that my children will always have You in their lives. They might stray, question, or have doubts, but You will not leave them. My children's children will have a chance to know You and to live for You. In the present I pray with thanksgiving for the grace You will extend in the future.

The Home Front

The Discipline of Discipline

He who listens to a life-giving rebuke will be at home among the wise.

PROVERBS 15:31

∽

I want my children to be counted among the wise as they grow older. Lord, help me ground them in Your truths as they face life's twists and turns. May they seek Your face in all circumstances. I pray for strength for myself and my husband as we discipline our children with life-giving instruction that comes from Your way, Your Word.

Let my children make their way in the world by making their home in Your kingdom. Infuse them with the riches of Your wisdom so they are armed with Your power each day of their lives...even those days that stretch beyond my lifetime. Thank You for hearing the pleas of a mother. My security is in You. I pray this is the legacy I will leave my children.

Staying True

I will walk in my house with blameless heart. I will set before my eyes no vile thing.

PSALM 101:2-3

✐

"Practice what you preach." This is an easy directive to espouse, but I catch myself wandering from its truth during my time away from home. God, I want to be consistent in character, yet I find myself walking a thin line when away from the watchful eyes of my family. It is convenient to toss a white lie out into the open when it saves time or preserves someone's pride. I blur the absolutes when I do not have the accountability of my children.

Lord, I pray to be an example in the way I live my life away from the home front. Let me enter my house with a blameless, pure heart. I do not want a double standard to crack the foundation I am building for my family. I thank You for the accountability I feel to my family and Your truth.

Finding My Way Home

Even the sparrow has found a home, and the swallow a nest for herself, where she may have her young—a place near your altar, O LORD Almighty, my King and my God.

PSALM 84:3

❧

As a child, I witnessed many different definitions of home. Some were not models of godliness or love, Lord. You know I entered into family life with a bit of hesitation. In my excitement to move into a future, I had moments of fear. How young I was in my faith then. I thought I was building a home on my own. Now I understand how You preserved me. You lifted me up when I was struggling. And You protected my nest and my young as I found my footing in Your wisdom.

My home is near the altar of Your heart. Guide everything I do or say within the circle of my family. I want us to draw near to You. And I want our hearts to become a home for You.

Open Heart, Open Home

Then they can train the younger women to love their husbands and children, to be self-controlled and pure, to be busy at home, to be kind, and to be subject to their husbands, so that no one will malign the word of God.

TITUS 2:4-5

❦

I can be intimidated by the younger generation, Lord. I could let this weakness continue, but it keeps me from opening up my home and my heart to those who need to hear about You. As my children grow older, may I seek ways to connect with them and their friends. I pray You will direct me toward a mentor relationship with young women.

I want to model Your love. Help me be humble and admit my imperfections. My past mistakes strengthen my testimony of Your grace. Let me serve You by encouraging young girls to become godly women.

Protection

Walking Under Your Protection

But let all who take refuge in you be glad; let them
ever sing for joy. Spread your protection over them,
that those who love your name may rejoice in you.

PSALM 5:11

∽

I rejoice in You, Lord. I celebrate my faith today. My clouds of sorrow have cleared, and I see the clear sky of Your face. I cannot hold back my song of thanksgiving. As I drive along the freeway, my usual anxiety and frustration is replaced by peace. I am walking under Your protection because I know and love Your name.

Forgive me for the many days I avoided Your refuge. My lips trembled with fear, yet I refused to move forward. I acted like a child resisting a mother's safe embrace. Now I run to You and the security You offer. The clouds might return, but my fear will not.

A Secure Shelter

You are my hiding place; you will protect me from trouble and surround me with songs of deliverance.

PSALM 32:7

∽

Life and love make us very vulnerable, Lord. The world's skyscrapers, mountains, and canyons cannot enclose an exposed soul. There is only one resting place for my spirit, and that is within Your encircled arms. I pray for Your hand to maneuver me through trouble. Push me past the cry of defeat and into the song of deliverance.

Do not let me hide from the challenges You bring my way. Destroy any excuses I create to avoid the trials set before me. You are not a reason to step away from difficulty. You are *the* reason to run to the fire so You may show Your faithfulness. You are my hiding place in this land of faulty shelters. Let my belief and perseverance be a testimony to Your goodness.

Watching Wisdom

Do not forsake wisdom, and she will protect you; love her, and she will watch over you.

PROVERBS 4:6

❧

Wisdom wears a yellow apron and the perfume of lavender. Wisdom is the image of a grandmother—surprisingly strong, faithful, all-knowing—with a soft voice that fills my head like no shout ever could. I am attentive in the presence of wisdom, Lord...Your wisdom. I sit in audience on the porch, awaiting a lesson for the day. I watch her moves closely because the space between words is the birthplace for truth.

Lord, help me take on the character of wisdom. May my children watch me closely and see Your mannerisms, Your love, Your actions between words. When my children lose their way, may they be led back to the presence of wisdom. She sits on the porch of Your heart.

The Safe Way

Discretion will protect you, and understanding will guard you.

PROVERBS 2:11

❧

Discretion is so rare; it has become an old-fashioned notion. We are all eager to move forward, to be on the cutting edge and spontaneous. Nobody wants to hold back when making a decision or a judgment. Lord, guide me in the use of discretion. Teach me the ways of the humble and shrewd. When You tell me to wait or hold my tongue, may I listen to You and understand the benefit.

I can be running forward with great certainty and see Your stop sign looming ahead. I don't often heed Your warning to slow down and be cautious. Let me learn from my past errors in judgment. Allow my actions to be calm and honorable instead of rash and irresponsible. I thank You for offering wisdom and discernment to those who follow Your directions.

Wonder

Blessed Vision

Many, O LORD my God, are the wonders you have done. The things you planned for us no one can recount to you; were I to speak and tell of them, they would be too many to declare.

PSALM 40:5

∽

Lord, the daily miracles I see so clearly are often lost on those who do not know You. I understand how privileged I am to be counted as one of Your own. I weep when I think of all the wonders I missed during my years of blindness. This is why I point out Your beauty and power to my children whenever I can. Until their hearts take hold of You with a firm grip of faith, I am their eyes, I am their witness, I am their guide.

Lord, when other people shrug at my claims of the miraculous infusing my daily routine, encourage me to continue sharing what I know as truth. I have been where they stand. I know that in the edge of their peripheral vision they see rays of Your light. My certainty shakes their doubt to its deceptive core. And they are that much closer to witnessing the wonders in their life.

Love Revealed

Show the wonder of your great love, you who save by your right hand those who take refuge in you from their foes.

PSALM 17:7

∽

When my children run to You, Lord (and I know they will one day soon), grant them the assurance You have given me. Shower Your love on them. They are at an advantage. Children exist in a world of wonder. Doubt rarely steals their belief when they need it. Their connection to Your loving presence is as natural as the bond between mother and child.

Will my children always look to the sky with delight and awe? Will stars always shine forth Your light and guide them to the birthplace of salvation? Will the winds of truth lead them to refuge? Lord, hear my prayers. When I am not able to point out Your marvels, may the miracles of Your hand rise up and make themselves known.

You Are Brilliant, Lord

LORD, I have heard of your fame; I stand in awe of your deeds, O LORD. Renew them in our day, in our time make them known; in wrath remember mercy.

HABAKKUK 3:2

In these times, the wonder of man's invention and seemingly independent success takes the limelight away from You. How easily we let go of what is true, forgetting who is in charge of our days. We watch the famous, rich, and powerful and think that surely they reached the pinnacle of society via their own devices. People hold on to this untruth because it implies their perfect destiny is as easily attained.

But faith shows us another side of life. The blessed catch a glimpse of Your glory on their way to claim their own, and there is no comparison. We see that the light cast from a secondary source is really powerless. But the light that comes from the true Light is life-giving, life-changing, and illuminates the only path to personal fulfillment.

Too Many to Count

He performs wonders that cannot be fathomed,
miracles that cannot be counted.

JOB 5:9

❧

One. Two. Three. Four. Fifty. Keeping track of Your miracles is something I can proudly say is no longer possible. There are too many to count. In my past I said, "I'm still waiting to see a miracle." That was when I was blind to Your wonders. My new vision of faith is one of the biggest miracles of all.

Lord, I am a humble servant kneeling before You. Your works are brilliant and amazing. How thankful I am to witness the mystery of Your goodness. I see Your hand in the simplest and most complex situations. I am stunned by Your grace in times of trial. My heart leaps with exuberance in times of joy. May my prayers of gratitude be as plentiful as the miracles I see today.

Discipline

Showing Mercy

Just as you who were at one time disobedient to God have now received mercy as a result of their disobedience, so they too have now become disobedient in order that they too may now receive mercy as a result of God's mercy to you. For God has bound all men over to disobedience so that he may have mercy on them all.

ROMANS 11:30-32

∽

My children—just like all of Your children—are going to be disobedient, Lord. Our fallible ways bring us full circle to Your mercy. I pray for a softened heart toward my children. May I bestow upon them grace and mercy in Your likeness. This is hard for me ... maybe because I do not feel allowed to make mistakes myself. Everyone depends on me to smooth the way. I carry a load that is unrealistic. And honestly, I take on too much responsibility out of guilt and a need for control, rather than a desire to serve.

Lord, I ask You to fill me with Your mercy. Until this gift affects me, I will carry a cross of martyrdom. And I will pass along to my children a negative attitude about following Your will. Change my motive for discipline from "works" to "faith" so that I may relinquish control and receive Your mercy.

Joy in Discipline

Buy the truth and do not sell it; get wisdom, discipline and understanding. The father of a righteous man has great joy; he who has a wise son delights in him.

PROVERBS 23:23-24

∽

When my patience is worn thin, I forget about the reserves of my Lord. It is my children who remind me to turn to You. Stuck in traffic and late for an appointment, I am thinking about the consequences of rescheduling and the domino effect of missing one item on my to-do list. But my children suggest we talk to You. There it is: wisdom coming forth from the little people strapped into car seats.

I thank You for their pure hearts. Their immediate response is to pray, to run to You and seek Your guidance. Lord, I rejoice in my children and their love for You. They lead this overly disciplined adult mind to the true source of life and wisdom: Your faithful presence.

Relying on Your Power

Our fathers disciplined us for a little while as they thought best; but God disciplines us for our good, that we may share in his holiness.

HEBREWS 12:10

❦

Lord, guide me in Your way. I was raised to know right from wrong, to be a good and fair person. But I still struggle with following a disciplined Christian life. I believe in the power of the cross. My spirit is not ruled by the law, but by Your power. Help me embrace Your holiness and lean not upon my understanding of the world, but upon Your knowledge of the way. You see what lies ahead for me and my family. I pray that I will trust the steps You show me.

God, create in me a disciplined heart that is not easily sidetracked. This busy life is packed with distractions, few of which are worthy of my time or Your time. I pray that I may fully experience the good of Your path.

Staying on the Path

*Be still before the LORD and wait patiently for him;
do not fret when men succeed in their ways, when
they carry out their wicked schemes.*

PSALM 37:7

౿

To continue on the way You have set before me
takes great control, Lord. Allow me to access You as my
Source of strength. I see new opportunities and want
to head toward them rather than stay disciplined along
this path. When a friend or associate achieves a level
of success I desire, my heart is covetous. Forgive me for
comparing my journey to that of another person.
Calm my spirit so I can wait for Your leading.

Your will takes me on a certain course. When I
grow lazy in my pursuit of the prize that awaits me,
please prod me forward. I do not want to be tempted
by a false joy. Inspire me to stay steadfast, disciplined,
and prepared to receive the blessings made just for me.

Order

The Cleansing Power of Peace

For God is not a God of disorder but of peace.

1 CORINTHIANS 14:33

∽

I want everything in order, Lord. I labor compulsively to keep up with my home, family, and work... and the pieces refuse to fall into place. This failure does not deter me. Yet I know the order I try to bring out of my chaos is a tidy version of truth—a worldly sense of perfection. It does not breathe peace into my soul and home. Only Your order does this.

When I am frantically cleaning my home instead of playing with my children, grant me Your order of importance. When I covet a neighbor's new car and yet do not give money to the needy, bring my sense of justice in line with Your way. This is my salvation.

Back to the Flock

As a shepherd looks after his scattered flock when he is with them, so will I look after my sheep. I will rescue them from all the places where they were scattered on a day of clouds and darkness.

EZEKIEL 34:12

❧

I have strayed from the protected hillside. My independent streak pushes me to the furthest ridge. Undaunted, I continue to wander down my slope of sinful ways. I tell myself that Your eyes are unable to follow me in the caverns, beneath the shelter of large stones. The narrow crevices are too small for You, surely.

But in a short time my legs grow weak, and I lose my footing. I am hungry, lost, and in danger. Now I pray that Your eyes will fall upon me. How I miss the security and order of my Shepherd's leading. I call out to You, eager to make known my hiding place. Lord, find this stray lamb. You are faithful. Smiling, You rescue me. I cling to You as You carry me home.

Order of Your Kingdom

Therefore, since we are receiving a kingdom that cannot be shaken, let us be thankful, and so worship God acceptably with reverence and awe, for our "God is a consuming fire."

HEBREWS 12:28-29

∽

Thanks to You, my life is set firmly on unshakable ground. No matter what comes my way, I stand on the rock of Your security. Fault lines spread out like fingers across the landscape of my life, but they do not stop my journey. Wind makes its boisterous way across the surrounding fields, tossing rootless life...but I do not change direction. Fires blush my cheeks with heat, but do not scorch my desire to continue.

In the midst of change and seasons of risk, Your command brings order to the chaos around me. My fears dissipate. Thank You, Lord, for the peace of Your enduring kingdom.

Preparing the Way

A voice of one calling: "In the desert prepare the way for the LORD; make straight in the wilderness a highway for our God."

ISAIAH 40:3

∾

The wilderness of my crazy existence is hardly an ideal environment for You. Yet I am trying to forge a road through the chaos to make room for Your passing. This is not easy for me. I have grown accustomed to the mess surrounding my heart and mind. Could You free me from my ties to all of this clutter? It is my love for You that insists upon this drastic change.

Your presence surrounds me. I turn to You for help and understanding. I must prepare a soul worthy of Your presence within. Make my thoughts pure. Transform my self-absorbed intentions into longings for the greater good. And make straight the road that leads my life to Your purpose.

Identity

Called by Name

*Lift your eyes and look to the heavens: Who created
all these? He who brings out the starry host one by
one, and calls them each by name.*

ISAIAH 40:26

✍

Lord, there is a kaleidoscope of roles I try to fill.
Mother. Wife. Friend. Neighbor. Each title offers many
new hats to wear. As I step into a role, I pray that You
are able to recognize *me* as the one You created.
Remove any false sense of self that lies within my soul.
May I walk along the path You have carved out of time
just for me.

Lord, You call the stars by name, and You will call
Your children home by name. Direct me according to
Your design. Today, I lay claim to the most important
identity of all: child of God.

Life's Accessories

*Your beauty should not come from outward adorn-
ment, such as braided hair and the wearing of gold
jewelry and fine clothes. Instead, it should be that of
your inner self, the unfading beauty of a gentle and
quiet spirit, which is of great worth in God's sight.*

1 PETER 3:3-4

∽

Lord, help me not buy into the concept of designer
lifestyles. I see how it distorts the value of people. Just
when I have a sense of my worth in Your eyes, I com-
pare my income, house, opportunities with those of
another person. I deceive myself into thinking these
are matters of importance. Do not let these deceptions
reach the hearts of my children.

Show me the beauty of my inner self—the part of
me that calls out to You and receives Your presence.
Silence the destructive voices that criticize my life.
Quiet my spirit so it can hear the love song You
whisper to my soul.

Knowing What Matters

What good is it for a man to gain the whole world,
and yet lose or forfeit his very self?

LUKE 9:25

∽

In this world of upgrades, "new and improved" products, and technological advancements, how do I show my children that they themselves are complete and perfect in You? They have learned to watch for the next big thing and do not understand the value of the here and now. God, may I speak words of encouragement to their hearts so they see significance in what they do today.

Lord, please give my children contentment. Let them savor gifts from You and not look beyond the current blessings. May their successes, large and small, turn their hearts to worship and praise. And may they never accept a substitute for the life of truth You grant them.

You Know My Soul

Yet you know me, O LORD; you see me and test my thoughts about you.

JEREMIAH 12:3

∽

My children think I am a mind reader when I predict their actions and reactions. I am able to do this because I know them so well. You know each of Your children on an even more intimate level. You see the scars we hide. You uncover the memories we bury. And You remove the sins we try to forget.

When I come to You with my bag of requests, worries, and questions, You are already familiar with these concerns. You know my every thought before it turns to action. You see my future with all its mistakes and triumphs. My whole identity is found in the One who made me. May my thoughts and the way I conduct myself represent You—the Creator who knows every part of me and *still* loves me.

Control

The Guiding Hand of Righteousness

When you were slaves to sin, you were free from the control of righteousness. What benefit did you reap at that time from the things you are now ashamed of? Those things result in death! But now that you have been set free from sin and have become slaves to God, the benefit you reap leads to holiness, and the result is eternal life.

ROMANS 6:20-22

❧

Sin can enter a heart or a home under the guise of freedom. Lord, do not let me or my family fall for this trap. When sin gives us flight, we can be sure we are soaring far from heaven's way. Eventually false wings tire, and we plummet to earth…dirty, broken, and far from the success we sought. I have experienced this place of loss, God. I know the pain of sin's control.

Lord, I want to embrace Your freedom. I want to don the wings of liberty. They lift me to new heights… a place where I can see through today's wants to Your kingdom. I give You control over my life, Lord, because this is the way to freedom.

Too Stubborn to Submit

Submit to one another out of reverence for Christ.

EPHESIANS 5:21

∽

Sometimes I am too stubborn to give in, Lord. Even when I see how it is the right thing to do. I refused to release my hold on a recent situation, and now I have regrets. Forgive me if I hurt the feelings of another person. Forgive me for modeling such a reluctant spirit to my children. Somehow submitting to You has been an easier concept to grasp than submitting to other people.

Help me, Lord. When I search my mind for all the reasons *not* to submit to another person, may You remind me what it means to serve in Your name. Break my spirit of control. Let me feel the weight of Your hand on my back as You teach me that by trusting other people, I am trusting You.

Giving It Over

*Submit to God and be at peace with him; in this
way prosperity will come to you.*

JOB 22:21

≈

I sense that I have held You back, Lord. I know You
are able to do all things. I don't really think I could stop
You from accomplishing anything. I don't always
partner with You like I should. I don't give You control
of the deepest places in my heart. Your power commands my respect. I witness Your faithfulness in the lives
of other people and in my own family. Still, I face You
while clenching a bag of situations, attitudes, and
dreams behind my back. Maybe You won't notice that
these pieces of my life are still in my possession, I
think to myself.

Forgive me for my ignorance, Lord. Today I will
reach into my bag of hang-ups and give You one...or
two. Be patient with me, Lord.

Letting the Spirit Take Charge

*You, however, are controlled not by the sinful nature
but by the Spirit, if the Spirit of God lives in you.*

ROMANS 8:9

∾

"The devil made me do it." As a believer, I do not take stock in this saying. Nonetheless, as a fallible human I have used it as an excuse for my careless actions. I might not say it to You directly, Lord. But I have relied on this misdirected blame to make myself feel better. It rarely works. And then I come to You, like now.

God, forgive me for my sins and my lack of personal control. I need to rely on the strength of the Spirit to guide my ways. You live in me. My all-powerful Lord is in charge of my soul, yet I try to handle situations with my own strength and purpose. Such a mistake! So I ask You, one more time, to place me under Your control and will. May I not look for excuses but always turn to You for grace.

Youth

You Lead the Young

*Since my youth, O God, you have taught me, and
to this day I declare your marvelous deeds.*

PSALM 71:17

∽

My stomach leaps into my throat while watching
my child play on a rickety playground swing or cross
a busy street after looking only one way first. I have to
remind myself of Your faithfulness back in my youth.
You were with me so many times when I was certain I
was running free and alone. When I was trying to stay
out of range of the eyes on the back of my mother's head,
You were right there beside me.

The fact that I am still alive is indeed Your marvelous
doing. Lord, give me faith to turn my children over to
You. Help me place the days of their youth in Your
protective care. Even with my superpowered mother
vision, I know there will be days when they venture far
from view, thinking they are alone, only to be guided
by their heavenly Father.

Restoring Youth

Praise the LORD, O my soul, and forget not all his benefits…who satisfies your desires with good things so that your youth is renewed like the eagle's.

PSALM 103:2,5

❧

Restore me, Lord. Give me back the pure desires that were born in my young heart so many years ago. I wanted to help people. I wanted to save the world. I was certain I could run the country. And I longed to become more like You. I was so passionate back then. But growing responsibilities, my progression into adulthood, and motherhood triggered the autopilot mechanism within me. I started just getting by.

I want to fly, Lord. I mean really fly. Toss me up in the air and make my stomach flip with passion and excitement. Let me feel the rush of gratitude that accompanies the fall back into Your arms. "Do it again!" One more time, Lord. I want to climb far above my current vantage point to see the many good things ahead. Have me soar so high that those on the ground look up and see the Master of the sky who commands the wind to lift my wings to new heights.

A Wise Child

Better a poor but wise youth than an old but foolish king who no longer knows how to take warning.

ECCLESIASTES 4:13

❧

I get so caught up in what I am supposed to do by society's standards that I miss the gentle leading of Your way. My children redirect me when they express their simple hearts that beat with Your perfect goodness. I am like the foolish king who barrels over and through situations with authority, yet makes decisions without wisdom. I am blinded by my seniority, forgetting that You are Lord over all.

Strip me of my royal cloak, the scepter, and the crown. These are false symbols on my being. They are the emblems of a king, and You are the only Ruler of this life, Lord. I come before You as a humble adult seeking Your direction. Transform me into a wise child of Your kingdom.

Covenant of My Youth

*Yet I will remember the covenant I made with you
in the days of your youth, and I will establish an ever-
lasting covenant with you.*

EZEKIEL 16:60

∽

I recall days of jumping on a trampoline. I could
experiment with twists, flips, and somersaults because
the cushioned landing assured me that my body
would never hit the hard ground. This is how I feel about
the covenant I have with You, Lord. You heard the
voice of a scared child long ago, and You answered
with Your grace and promises to hold me up for eternity.

I know hard times will be a part of my life, but I
trust You every step—and jump—of the way. Don't let
me become someone who is so jaded that I only trust
You when things are smooth and perfect. I want to be
one of Your disciples, Lord. I want to say, "I accept this
and wait upon Your leading," even when I am uncertain how I will land.

Purpose

A Path of Purpose

Because God wanted to make the unchanging nature of his purpose very clear to the heirs of what was promised, he confirmed it with an oath.

HEBREWS 6:17

≪∕≫

I see love as Your purpose, Lord. Is that right? I cannot begin to presume I understand all that You know, but I do understand Your Word. I see how the message of love penetrates all that I read. I try to bring this into my life by showing compassion to other people. I try to give it back to You through efforts at service and kindness.

Do I show You love as I should? Do You call me to a deeper commitment and level of service? I want to be consistent in my representation of You. I long to be an heir of Your promises and Your future. Bring me to a place of understanding and purpose, Lord. Once I accept Your oath, I can follow the path.

True Calling

With this in mind, we constantly pray for you, that our God may count you worthy of his calling, and that by his power he may fulfill every good purpose of yours and every act prompted by your faith.

2 THESSALONIANS 1:11

∽

Faith breeds purpose. I have seen this in my life, Lord. When I encounter those who seem so very lost or hopeless, I pray for them. I remember what it was like to have nothing beyond my immediate circumstances. Then You came along and opened my eyes to life beyond life.

You are the Fulfiller of dreams. You meet us where we are and pave the way to eternity. Lord, I thank You for Your commitment to my life. Aim my objectives toward Your will. Thank You for weeding out my false starts and unproductive efforts and leading me toward a true calling.

Recess

Real Laughter

Sarah said, "God has brought me laughter, and everyone who hears about this will laugh with me." And she added, "Who would have said to Abraham that Sarah would nurse children? Yet I have borne him a son in his old age."

GENESIS 21:6-7

∽

Miracles do happen, Lord. I am not telling You anything You don't know. But today I reflect on how amazing Your acts of grace and greatness are in my daily life. I look at my children and instantly remember every moment of their births, how the wonder of it all consumed me. I think of Sarah and the unimaginable miracle of her motherhood at such an old age. You are such a good God.

When faced with the oddities of life and the nobody-will-believe-this moments, I laugh with deep joy. What else can I do? I really think You are playful. You created fellowship with us. Thank You, Lord, for a full relationship...one including laughter, joy, pain, and celebration.

Dreams Come True

When the LORD brought back the captives to Zion, we were like men who dreamed. Our mouths were filled with laughter, our tongues with songs of joy.

PSALM 126:1-2

∽

I like to ask my children what they have dreamed as soon as they awaken. I find it fascinating how our minds soar to different places and experiences as we slumber. The dreams I have while I am awake relate to happiness, health, and justice. And I take them to You, Lord, in my times of prayer during the day. These precious minutes are my respite from work, routine, and trouble. It takes just a moment in Your presence, and I am filled with great joy.

Only You can bring me back to contentment from a path of frustration. Only You offer a never-ending source of fulfillment. Best of all, You are the Maker of my dreams-come-true. And when I awaken from moments of great joy, I want to tell You everything.

When Today Lacks Joy

You have made known to me the path of life; you will fill me with joy in your presence, with eternal pleasures at your right hand.

PSALM 16:11

✍

I would not want to repeat the mornings I have had lately, Lord. They have been filled with tears and unexpected arguments with the children. All of a sudden our routine seems to rub them wrong. Forgive me for being so ready to wave good-bye to their little faces so that I can turn to You and cry for a while. Your presence not only calms me and releases me from the tension, but You also replace my sorrow with joy...true joy...the kind that stays with me during the rest of the day. I can even laugh about my bad mornings.

I can only imagine how wonderful it will be to reside in Your presence throughout eternity, how You will still our spirits with a whispered word. And I imagine You will remind us of our earthly days. And we will laugh over the little troubles that brought us running to Your lap for comfort.

My Soul Worships You

Sing to him a new song; play skillfully, and shout for joy.

PSALM 33:3

∽

My voice may not play a pretty tune, Lord, but I do sing loudly for Your benefit. I let my feet dance, skip, and wander about the house as I shout out my version of a joyful song. I think this is pleasing to You. I hope it is. Somehow this acting out gives me permission to feel Your joy more deeply. I open up my vocal chords and my heart simultaneously, and Your delight flows through me … every bit of me.

I should let joy wash over me more often. I have become so rigid, so proper, so careful of my steps and my words. Help me get over myself when I am too serious, Lord. It is through moments of pure happiness that I truly worship You.

Rebellion

Return of the Rebellious Spirit

Remember not the sins of my youth and my rebellious ways; according to your love remember me, for you are good, O LORD.

PSALM 25:7

༄

I am embarrassed to think of the many sins I have committed over my lifetime. So much weakness. For years I was rebellious, and now and then that same spirit comes over me. Lord, please save me from the anger that can make everything around me turn shades of black. I miss the wonder of Your world when I let problems turn me against You.

Look upon this child of Yours with love, Lord. I think of the times when I sought Your will and truly abided by Your Word. I pray those times are more common than naught. Give me strength to follow Your voice as it sings life into my soul. You free me.

Getting Back to Your Light

There are those who rebel against the light, who do not know its ways or stay in its paths.

JOB 24:13

∽

On particularly bad days, Lord, Your hope shines through my blinds in the morning, and I do not welcome it. I want to wallow in my anger or self-pity. I don't care if I am ugly, disheveled, and antagonistic to those around me. My stubborn spirit pushes me away from Your light. I don't always feel worthy of Your love.

No matter how much I resist Your grace, Lord, don't give up on me. You know I am scared. You know there are days when I do not even know how to rise up out of my apathy. Reach for me. Seek me, Lord. Even in my rebellion, the power of my Savior's love seeps into my bones and becomes a part of me. Lord, I might start out kicking and screaming, but I long to step into Your radiance and be carried in Your arms.

Working with You

*Far be it from us to rebel against the LORD and turn
away from him today by building an altar for burnt
offerings, grain offerings and sacrifices, other than
the altar of the LORD our God that stands before his
tabernacle.*

JOSHUA 22:29

∽

I work hard to create a great home for my family.
You see the effort that I make and the desire I have to
build a life. Sometimes this passion is so strong I fight
You for control of these blessings. How counterpro-
ductive! Is it pride? A lack of faith? Tell me, Lord. And
help me overcome my areas of rebellion.

I pray I never mold these blessings into ungodly
altars. I give this life back to You with a trusting spirit.
To be Your faithful servant, I need to do this. Give me
strength. Let me begin each day with prayers of thanksgiving and a renewed commitment to make every
word and deed and accomplishment an offering to
You.

Strength for the Race

*I have fought the good fight, I have finished the race,
I have kept the faith.*

2 TIMOTHY 4:7-8

‿

The same strong spirit that is within me is definitely in my children. I see myself in their actions and attitudes. I hear myself repeat my parents' words of warning and correction on a daily basis. Lord, in those moments when I am frustrated and pray desperately for patience and peace, help me to see the positive aspects of their natures.

Remind me of my past trials. Let me see how at each of my low points, my strong spirit kept me determined in my faith. I persevered and fought the good fight. Next time I am in a standoff with my kids, turn my despair into celebration. Help me embrace their strengths. I know doing this will serve them and You well.

Falling Down

When I Stumble

The LORD is my light and my salvation—
whom shall I fear?
The LORD is the stronghold of my life—
of whom shall I be afraid?

PSALM 27:1

∽

I cower at the sight of certain insects. Heights send fear shivers down my spine. And I was afraid of the dark for so long as a child. In these situations, I have relied on Your Word to see me through, Lord. Now when I calm the fears of my children, I share Psalm 27:1. When I face uncertain risk or known troubles I return to the stronghold of my life—my faith in You.

I pray my children will always seek Your strength in times of worry and anxiety. May my example lead them to Your feet when fear enters their lives. As for me, I will rely on Your light to find my footing when fear causes me to stumble.

Why Do I Doubt Your Help?

He went in and said to them, "Why all this commotion and wailing? The child is not dead but asleep." But they laughed at him.

MARK 5:39-40

❧

I have laughed at You before—in Your face, even. I am not proud of this, Lord. I don't recognize I am doing this until remorse and regret set in. When I fall to the deepest depths of sorrow or confusion, You promise hope will come, healing will come. But I resist hearing these words of truth. It is as if I cannot believe one more time, though You have always been faithful. I laugh to protect myself from being hurt.

Why does hardship harden my heart and cause doubt to replace what I know to be true? Lord, please remove this behavior from my ways. When my brokenness refuses to believe Your promises will be fulfilled, my spirit is crying out to You, "Please prove me wrong, Lord."

Humble Worship

Who is wise and understanding among you? Let him show it by his good life, by deeds done in the humility that comes from wisdom.

JAMES 3:13-14

∽

I was flat on my face, Lord. You saw me. I was caught in a very humbling situation. Thank goodness I had enough wisdom to accept it, to regain an upright position, and to bask in the glory of humiliation. As it should be, the glory was Yours, not mine. And I gave credit where credit was due. Accepting the situation reflected Your grace.

I thank You for these opportunities, Lord. Really. If I controlled the world (or at least my slice of it), I would never humble myself. Pride consumes me in my quest to look like I have my act together. Forgive me for such pride. Give me wisdom and the good life...the one that includes humility. And next time I am flat on my face, may I use this convenient position to bow down and worship You.

Slow Motion

Reach down your hand from on high; deliver me and rescue me from the mighty waters, from the hands of foreigners whose mouths are full of lies, whose right hands are deceitful.

PSALM 144:7-8

∽

I am slipping, Lord. A little bit each day I drift toward depression and unhappiness. I am believing the world's lies again. I diminish the value of my life and my family each time I nod in submission to deception. I reach up for Your hand. Please rescue me from the confusion of sorrow.

Lord, see me in my time of trouble. I am not strong enough to do this on my own. I am well-practiced at falling, but still struggle with asking for help. So please, Lord, hear my cries. Only You can rescue me.

Why?

Asking Questions

*My God, my God, why have you forsaken me? Why
are you so far from saving me, so far from the
words of my groaning? O my God, I cry out by day,
but you do not answer, by night, and am not silent.*

PSALM 22:1-2

❧

Why are You distant when I need You here beside
me? My situation requires Your attention. I hear
silence. For days I have waited for Your acknowledg-
ment. Lord, do You roam the heavens preoccupied
with the needs of other people and Your own concerns? Meet me here right now in my time of need.

I am throwing a tantrum. I know it. I wouldn't
blame You if You refused to listen to my shout of
despair. I question You because I am so desperate. In
the stillness of my soul, I know better. I sense the dis-
tance is my doing. In my anger, I have closed off my
spirit to Your words of comfort and salvation. Silence
my accusations, Lord. My screams of neglect are
drowning out Your answer of mercy.

Still the Storms Within

He replied, "You of little faith, why are you so afraid?" Then he got up and rebuked the winds and the waves, and it was completely calm.

MATTHEW 8:26

✍

My steps of faith are quite wobbly, as though I have been out to sea for too long. In a way, this is true. The pace of my life causes me to lose sight of my Rock, my Shore—You. I have nothing to anchor me to truth and understanding. Discernment flows away with the hazardous current, and I am left questioning You and Your presence.

Heal my unbelief, Lord. Cease the torrential rains of fear that blind me. I want to see Your face as Your direction silences the thunder, parts the clouds, and calms my spirit. You who created all of nature…all of me…are worthy of my trust. Let me walk steadily to Your arms.

Hearing Your Response

Why do you call me, "Lord, Lord," and do not do what I say? I will show you what he is like who comes to me and hears my words and puts them into practice.

LUKE 6:46-47

∽

I ask You this, Lord: Why does her life seem so great? Everything works out for her. Even in hard times she somehow surfaces stronger and more certain of Your love.

You give me the same answer every time. Her life models the relationship You long to have with me. She asks and receives. When I say, "Lord, Lord" and relay my list of troubles, I am venting, not asking for guidance. My clenched fists are never opened up to receive Your wisdom and grace. Let me really hear Your instruction and be disciplined to follow. I don't want this conversation to be one-sided anymore.

Figuring Out Your Mysteries

Beyond all question, the mystery of godliness is great: He appeared in a body, was vindicated by the Spirit, was seen by angels, was preached among the nations, was believed on in the world, was taken up in glory.

1 TIMOTHY 3:16

∽

My children ask me why about every little thing they see and experience. It is their nature to desire understanding. Have I lost my desire to ask You questions? Do I glide on through my life without seeking true understanding? I should be consumed by my desire to understand Your mystery, Lord.

I do not question You or Your existence, yet I have many unanswered questions about life, heaven, death, and the future my children will have. Can I come to You with these inquiries? I pray that You will receive these questions. I am Your child … it is my way.

Fulfillment

*The LORD will fulfill his purpose for me; your love,
O LORD, endures forever—do not abandon the
works of your hands.*

PSALM 138:8

∾

In my early days of faith, the expectations I placed
upon You were plenty. I depended on You for everything. I dared not take a step without Your direction.
Now I lean toward self-sufficiency sometimes, but I
know of Your faithfulness. Bring me back to a state of
dependency on You for my every move.

Without You I have no purpose. I invented various
meanings for my life before I met You, but those plans
were ways to pass time. Your way offers the design of
a master plan. I am so blessed to be Your child, Lord.
I am in Your hands, and I long to be molded into the
person You want me to become. Oh, how You have sur-
passed my expectations. You grant my soul purpose. You
give my life reason. And You fill my eternity with
hope.

Books You Can Believe In
HARVEST HOUSE PUBLISHERS

One-Minute Prayers™

This collection of simple, heartfelt prayers and Scriptures is designed to serve the pace and needs of everyday life. Offering renewal, this prayer journey encourages readers to experience fellowship with God during busy times.

The Power of a Praying® Woman

Stormie Omartian

Stormie has led nearly two million women into deeper, more fulfilling prayer lives. In *The Power of a Praying® Woman,* through her knowledge of Scripture and candid examples of her own epiphanies in prayer, she shows you how to

- draw closer to God
- know His plans and purposes for your life
- receive comfort, help, and strength for every day

Trust Him moment by moment with the concerns of your heart and discover the awesome power prayer will release in *your* life.